ACKNOWLEDGEMENTS:
The assistance of the Leisure Committee of N. W. L. District Council
Mantle Community Arts
Mantle Oral History Project

Interviews and research: Robert Walker, Tracey Roberts, Colin Hyde and Jeanne Carswell

Typing: Colin Hyde
Typesetting: Steve Duckworth

Special thanks to Mr E K Deeming for the loan of photographs and Mr John Knight for his enthusiasm

Printed by Rural Press

Published by:
Coalville Publishing Company Ltd
The Springboard Centre
Coalville
Leicester
LE6 4DR

© Copyright Coalville Publishing Company & Mantle Oral History Project 1991
ISBN 1 872479 05 7

CINEMA IN COALVILLE

Edited by Jeanne Carswell and Tracey Roberts

The Golden Age of the cinema and big screen entertainment brought daily queues of people to the area around Marlborough Square, to the Grand, The Regal and the Rex. When Edward K Deeming announced the closure of the Rex in 1984, it was the end of the Deeming family's long association with cinema in Coalville.

The following recollections are taken from tape recorded interviews with Coalville residents who remember, in their own words, more than seventy years of cinemagoing.

Some dates:

Coalville Electric Theatre — opened circa 1910
became the Grand Cinema — 22 November 1920
became the Grand Ballroom — 23 September 1954 (sold to Mecca 16 January 1973)

Olympia Roller Skating Rink — opened circa 1908
became the Olympia Picture House circa 1910
demolished and rebuilt as the Regal Cinema — opened 2 November 1933
became the Coalville Casino club — 19 April 1963

The Rex Cinema — opened 2 February 1938
became Rex 1 and Rex 2 — May 1973
closed — 3 May 1984

I was born in Coalville, virtually in the cinema because the flat attached to the Grand Cinema was called Marlborough House but was really part and parcel of the main auditorium of the cinema.

My father had come into town in 1920. His first effort after leaving the army (he was in the Tank Corps) was in the Potteries and he bought a small cinema called 'Talk of the Hill'. It wasn't at all successful; he was looking for some better place to come to and fortunately he found Coalville.

The cinema which was known as the Coalville Electric Theatre was owned by a Mr. Johnson who'd started some major alterations to the old building, which was possibly opened around 1910. After purchase by my father he completed the alterations and reopened it as the Grand Cinema on 22nd November 1920.

It remained a very successful cinema until the beginning of the Second World War when it was closed down and used as a food store.

E K Deeming

The films were very jumpy before the First World War. They were mostly Cowboys and Indians, nearly every one. There was a place called the Olympia and they'd got a dynamo of their own and they had lights. Outside it said, 'Olympia' lit up in lights.

A College

Coalville Electric Theatre, opened circa 1910.

The cinema was popular but we were only allowed to go to the cinema on Saturday, for the Saturday matinee. I think it was about a penny ha'penny to get in, and they gave an orange! We saw Tom Mix and Laurel and Hardy.

It was all wooden seats and there was no music on the film, there used to be some woman play the piano to suit the film.

W.H.Windebank

I can remember Dr. Fu Manchu. Every time he came on I used to hide behind the seat because he was a Chinaman with great long fingernails and he used to frighten me to death. That was the silent films and a lady played the piano, but that was at the Olympia.

P.Palmer

> COALVILLE – ELECTRIC. – The enterprise of the management of this most comfortable place of entertainment afforded on Friday excellent views of the Coronation Procession, the pictures being as distinct as they were varied. It was aptly stated in the streamers announcing the bill that there was no need for a tiresome journey to London to see the Coronation Procession. The colliery area is indebted to the management, and good houses are assured. Apart from the Royal Procession pictures, there were other interesting films. The theatre, known of old as the Public Hall, carried off honours for decoration on Coronation Day, and no place, public building or private, in the area could have excelled the charming front with electric devices, which crowds journeyed to see in Marlborough Square during the week. The manager was deservedly congratulated.

Extract from THE STAGE June 29, 1911.

Coalville Electric Theatre. Decorated for the coronation of George V, 1911.

The owners of cinemas could sense that people had come out to enjoy the fancy world of the cinema and a higher standard of comfort and heating than they would be getting in their homes. I think from that point of view, the cinema served a social purpose in the 1920s and 1930s.

E K Deeming

The Grand....we went there to the pictures. I can remember us having to stand all one night. I used to go with my sister when it was my day off. But I always had to be in at ten o'clock, always, it didn't matter where I went. We'd get our tickets and if there was some fellows we knew, we'd talk to them.

E Hoden

The first time we went to the cinema was when Al Jolson's film came to Coalville. I'd be about fifteen then, I should think. There was penny seats, tuppenny seats and fourpenny seats. Sometimes we used to crawl along the floor and get into the 'fourpennies' when we'd only paid a penny.

P Palmer

The Electric, followed by the Grand showed films, the Pathe News, then a two reel comedy followed by the serial and finally, a feature film. The two reel comedies starred famous names like Charlie Chaplin, Buster Keaton, Harry Langdon, Ben Turpin, Chester Conklin, Stan Laurel (many years before he teamed up with Oliver Hardy), Harold Lloyd and the Keystone Cops. The serials were often twenty-six instalments always ending with the hero or heroine in a dreadful situation. We could scarcely wait until the next week to see if they got out of it safely. They always did!

Films often broke and if there was much delay in making a repair there would be lots of booing, whistling and stamping of feet. I think we used to judge a film not so much on its content but on how much it suffered or was free from 'raining'. The stream of lines and flickers running down the picture could be most irritating and when people were asked what the film was like the reply often was, "Not very good, it was raining too much." A piano accompanied the films, the pianist looking up at the screen to determine the mood of the music.

G Lowe

Of course there were all the breakdowns you had to allow for. Often the film would break down and then there'd be a great clapping and shouting and booing and screaming until they got the projector working again. If you didn't get a break down at least once a month, it wasn't Coalville cinema!

It caused a bit of fun amongst the audience and the kids loved it. You went there to boo and shout when the film broke down.

M Sparrow

The Grand Cinema was run on very nice lines. It had an eight-piece orchestra, under a man named Williamson. It was silent cinema, of course, until the end of the 1920s. Round about 1928, Western Electric installed talkie equipment.

It was a one-floor cinema, there was no balcony. It booked seats, especially at the weekend. On Saturdays when there were two houses every seat was booked. Prices were commensurate with people's pockets — for sixpence, ninepence, a shilling, perhaps one-and-three if you booked your seat. This price structure ran through for a long period, from the mid 1920s until well into the 1930s, I imagine.

E K Deeming

POST CARD

CORRESPONDENCE — ADDRESS ONLY

F. E. Mays & Co. Marlboro Studio, Coalville

1. C Bunn
2. Mary Beale
3. H. Whiteman
4.
5. H Jacobs
6. C Jacobs
7. E. V. Rowell
8. J Watson
9. S. Haywood
10. G. A. Beniston
11. E. Ingall

12. E. Ingall
13. Jas Essex
14. J Bowler
15.
16. Chas K Deeming
17. Barbara
18. D. Deeming
19. J H Buxton
20. EDDIE
21. Laura Beddow
22. J E Wright

23. W. G Ball
24. E. C Grundy
25. Wilf Lickling
26. T. Wright
27. Albert Williams
28.
29. T Gunney
30. T Goddard
31. Horace Bott
32. H Williams

Cinema staff outing 1928

They used to come around with ice-creams I can remember, but we were lucky if we'd got enough money to go to the pictures let alone pay for anything else, even when I was working.

E Hoden

The Saturday matinees would be particularly well supported. Even though one expected the crowds of children to be big enough, frequently there was an additional bonus because every child would receive an orange. There was a very handy greengrocer's next door to the Grand called Bartrams. There must have been enormous trouble in the cinema for cleaning up afterwards.

E K Deeming

They had ice-cream and pop. The usherette brought them round and stood at the front with a tray, that was the usual. At the interval, they had a sort of counter where they sold ice-cream and pop cartons. But that's all I remember at the Coalville cinema. I can't remember them selling anything else, not like they did later on, in a little shop. It was just what the usherette brought round in a tray.

M Sparrow

My early schoolboy memories of the Grand cinema are of a wonderful place I used to go back to for the afternoon matinee on a Monday. That would start at 4.30, suitable for children coming home from school. I had my place, about four rows from the back and a friend would be with me probably. From the flat which was attached to the cinema the maid would bring down a tray of tea and cakes and buns, and pikelets sometimes, and we would eat these solidly right through what would be the comedy, or the serial, and she'd come and clear them away before the main picture started.

E K Deeming

Safety curtain with local advertisements — the Olympia.

As a child you went every Saturday to the pictures and it cost tuppence. We had monkey nuts and an orange and a piece of elastic and you peeled your orange and you shot with the elastic at the screen if you didn't like it.

E Boulstridge

At the children's matinees they used to have these pea-shooters and if you weren't careful you got one in the eye. If you said anything to 'em they'd just get the pea-shooter and shoot you! I used to go round with the ice-cream tray and by the time I'd finished my tray was full of dried peas.

Anon

The great strength of the cinema, and it's the great strength of its economic success in the 1920s and 1930s, was that virtually every film was suitable for family audiences. There was no such thing as 'parental guidance' films or 'X' films, and people did come week after week to the cinema.

I suppose Elstree helped, but it was really the strength of Hollywood that the films being turned out could almost all be viewed by Mum and Dad, and the family as well, without any offence being given.

Charlie Chaplin was immensely popular although I understand from my father that he always struck a very hard bargain with the cost of his films. The big flamboyant stars like Jean Harlow and Clark Gable were stars of a class which we don't know today, because people would go to see a film on the strength of that man's or that woman's name on the poster outside.

In the 1920s and 1930s stars tended to be type-cast and they didn't risk a star's reputation in a subject which was wholly unsuitable for them. People liked that. They didn't like to be surprised too much by the character which was being played by the star they adored.

The Olympia, 1930s.

The closure of the cinema in 1940, to be taken over as a foodstore, was disappointing to the regulars because the people who came into the cinema tended to be regulars and you could recognise them coming in every week, whatever the programme. There wasn't a great show of preference for films. People would tend to come to the same seat on the same night every week.

During the 1920s the opposition to the Grand cinema was the Olympia. The Olympia picture house at the other end of Marlborough Square had originally been a roller-skating rink, round about 1908. It became a picture house, possibly around 1910. It was purchased by my father in the late 1920s and continued to run as a cinema but plans by then were being arranged for a new super-cinema to be built in the great cinema building era of the 1930s. It was demolished and became the Regal cinema and opened on 2nd November 1933.

E K Deemimg

Demolition of the Olympia circa 1933.

There was a tale years ago that during the war the cinema reels were shared by Whitwick, Coalville and Ibstock, in that order. The film would be started off at Whitwick and then a chap on his cycle would bike like mad to Coalville to deliver the reel and then wait there, and on to Ibstock. How they got the second reel there...there must have been two chaps. Apparently one night, during the blackout, this was happening. One reel was going from one cinema to another and there was an air-raid siren and the chap took refuge in a ditch with the reel and his bicycle. We don't know whether it ever did get to the next cinema or not.

There were two cinemas in Coalville, the Rex and the Regal. It was a case of going to queue. The queues would be right up Margaret St. or right round the corner into Owen St. We used to do what we called queue hopping. If you were with a group, half the group would stay in one cinema queue, the other half would be in the other queue and as you got nearer to the door the ones that were further away would hop out and join the others so we at least got into one cinema and we weren't turned away. Mr. Deeming used to act as commissionaire on the doors to keep an eye on the queues but we used to slip by him.

M Sparrow

Mr. Gooding was the general manager and his wife used to be in the paybox. He used to manage at the Regal and I've heard that there was great competition at that time — I don't know whether it was true — between Mr. Gooding and the manager at the Rex to get the most people in. If he was starting the matinee at 2.30 at the Rex, Gooding would start at 2.00 at the Regal to get them in.

J Knight

Queuing outside the Regal Cinema.

There used to be two houses and you weren't allowed to go to the second house and you weren't out of work early enough to go to the first house.

Anon

Every month a new programme came out. It was a folded card with all the films on for the month. Monday, Tuesday, Wednesday, would be one film, then it would change on Thursday, Friday, Saturday, and again on Sunday for the special show. So that meant you went three times a week and you saw a different film. Sunday show was a one-off film, something special, only shown on a Sunday. I think there was only one performance on a Sunday.

The problem was if it was a long film. The last bus for home left Coalville at ten o'clock. Sometimes the film would run over, perhaps until twenty past ten, and you missed the end. There's lots and lots of films that I never did see the end of. You wondered, how did it end? Did it end happy ever after?

I think there were colour films then, but most seemed to be in black and white — they were the good old films, the real tear jerkers. There was one — I never did see the end of it — a true story film called 'The Well'. It was about a little girl named Kathy who fell down a well and it happened in America. I remember it being on the news. I presume they got the child out but it was a very sad film. It was just the fight to get the child out of the well and how they did it. That was one film I really do remember.

M Sparrow

There are two factors involved in booking films for a cinema in Coalville. We had complete access to all films on offer and the film renters would send a list perhaps every month or two months showing what new films were available. Then there is the factor of what is suitable for Coalville. Every audience, every town, tended to have a favourite type of picture, one which they would go to more than another type. One doesn't want to be cynical but perhaps the type

Marlborough Square, showing the Regal Cinema.

of films which went well in Coalville wouldn't go well in Leamington. They would be more of a hearty, action, dangerous type — nothing too sophisticated in the area of art films or continental films. Frequently the booker, which would be my father or me, would make a great mistake.

E K Deeming

I remember once, going to see a film with a couple of friends and my boyfriend at the time, and it was all knockouts in boxing. The cinema was in uproar! I have never seen people standing up in a cinema, shouting, and sort of punching each other and getting so excited. It was just like a football match! I can just remember that being such an exciting film. I don't know what it was called or anything, it was just all major knockouts in title fight boxing. It was rip-roaring stuff and we'd never had one like that before.

M Sparrow

In the silent days, and well into the 1930s, films were invariably bought on a flat rate. The film distributor would come along to my father's office, or he'd go to Birmingham, to the renter's offices, and they'd strike a price for that film. It could be anywhere between £1-10s and £8 to £10 for a really big one.

Later it was realised by the distributors that sometimes they were not getting their fair share and so the percentage terms came into play. It meant very often that a film would be booked at 25%, which is normally the rock bottom, of the net takings at the box office. They didn't take the ice-cream takings or chocolate or cigarettes, just a percentage of the initial ticket revenue at the box office. With a really big picture, such as 'Gone with the Wind', the percentage could be as much as fifty percent. Never over that, fifty percent was the top. Until the 1960s and 1970s, when it moved between 50% and 75%, and there was a great haggling over this!

E K Deeming

The Grand Cinema circa 1927

THE RE

The Rex opened in 1938. It was a civic occasion, the Chairman of the Council came. All the openings tended to run the same, with the people on the stage giving speeches. The stars didn't turn up to Coalville but sent telegrams instead. The studios would send congratulation cards.

E K Deeming

THE INAUGUR

WEDNESDAY, F

at

Prog

1. Grand Opening Ceremony
3. News
5. "The Charge of

ERROL FLYNN and
(Stage Prologue b

God Sav

K CINEMA

AL CEREMONY

RUARY 2nd, 1938

p.m.

mme

2. God Save The King
4. Trees (A Rhapsody in Colour)

the Light Brigade"

IVIA DE HAVILLAND
Mr. Fred Forgham)

The King

It was Wednesday afternoon and the film was 'The Charge of the Light Brigade'. As you walked in that cinema it was beautiful, all red plush seats and red curtains. It was really marvellous with all the councillors there giving speeches. Then they showed the film. It was quite a nice afternoon.

Anon

COALVILLE'S MAGNIFICENT BALLROOM
MR. C. K. DEEMING'S ENTERPRISE

Mr. C. K. Deeming's ability to pursue an idea to a successful conclusion was again exemplified at last Thursday evening's official opening of the new Grand Ballroom at Coalville. This achievement is something of which both he and the town may well be proud.

But with after 34 years' association with him, Coalville people are — quite understandably — apt to take it for granted that whatever Mr. Deeming undertakes will be of a high standard. This ballroom is as much in advance of anything Coalville has hitherto experienced, in the way of dancing facilities, as were his innovations brought into local cinema entertainment, way back in the 'twenties....the purchase and re-construction of the old Palace Electric Theatre, with its re-opening as "The Grand" Cinema, in 1920; the acquisition of "The Olympia" skating rink (1927); its conversion and eventual demolition to make room for the present "Regal" (1933); and the erection of "The Rex" Cinema (1938)

PLANNED IN PRE-WAR DAYS

This idea of converting "The Grand" into a ballroom and banqueting hall was planned in pre-war days, but the exigencies of the 1939-45 conflict necessitated its being shelved. For several years it was in use as a Ministry of Food storage, and not until January of this present year were the necessary licences issued to enable the work of transformation to proceed. It is almost an incredible transformation: not one of the hundreds who have already visited it on or since opening night would recognise the building at all!

There is a ballroom, capable of accommodating anything between 400 and 600 dancers: with floor of Malayan Kempas; the lighting, which is claimed to be the most spectacular in the county; and a general magnificence and size which would do credit to any town, anywhere.

Throughout the building, there is efficient air-conditioning and heating, and every conceivable facility has been installed for the comfort and convenience of patrons. In addition to the "top bar" there is a buffet, with up to date kitchen accommodation and facilities for dinner-dances and other special functions.

CONSIDERABLE OUTLAY

All this has entailed a very considerable outlay — much more than the original £12,000 estimated cost: a very tangible proof of Mr. Deeming's faith in the soundness of his idea in providing for Coalville an amenity on such a really lavish scale. He is certain that Coalville and district will make response.

The premises are to be available for lettings. Even before the building was completed there were quite a number of bookings arranged for special nights, by various organisations.

A real cross-section of the local public was present at Thursday's opening night — an attendance of 400, of which, about 100 were friends from Loughborough. Factories, sports clubs, associations, Chamber of Trade, Rotary, and other organisations were represented.

The actual opening was a happy, informal ceremony, presided over by Mr. Edward Knight Deeming (son of Mr. C. K. Deeming) who is well-known both to Loughborough and Coalville audiences, and who will supervise the management of the new ballroom. In extending a cordial welcome to the company, Mr. Deeming said that the very best had been put into the preparation of the ballroom, and it was now up to the public to justify the faith which had been placed in them by his father and himself.

"A MANGROVE TREE"

The opening ceremony was performed by Brig. Gen. R. S. Abbott, of Castle Rock, chairman of the local bench of magistrates. He said that Coalville had often reminded him of a mangrove tree — throwing fresh shoots all over the place, but developing nothing at the centre. But, with this ballroom, they now had an ambitious project situated right in the heart of the town.

The Brigadier continued: Coalville was indeed lucky to have a man such as Charles K. Deeming in their midst, his capabilities and achievements were well-known to them all. Everyone would join in wishing him the utmost success in this, his latest venture.

Mr. C. K. Deeming made appropriate acknowledgement.

Supporting the Brigadier were Mrs. Abbott, Mrs. Barbara Walker, Mr. S. W. Milburn, and Mr. Nicholas C. Moss.

A dance programme followed, to the music of Smilin' Johnnie Smith and his "Out of the Blue" orchestra.

Extract from the Coalville Times — September 1954.

The Olympia, during demolition to make way for the Regal.

I went to the Cinema Ball once. If you wasn't on duty you could go but the cinema had to be kept open. Everybody had an invite. The usherettes and families, the cleaners and the projectionists, the managers and under managers. It was quite a do really, we had refreshments and there was the band and dancing.

Anon

The staff were invited but it was really to raise funds for the Cinematograph Trades Benevolent Fund which had been in operation since the 1930s. We tried very hard to get a star or a starlet to come down for it. Barbara Windsor came once. Stanley Baker came once for fifty pounds — cash in hand.

E K Deeming

The first annual cinema ball, 11th March 1955.

The Grand had an excellent dance floor but we could also set up tables for dinner dances so many local firms used it – Pegson's Grieves, Clutsom and Kemp. We had two hundred people seated sometimes.

E K Deeming

I went about twenty years ago. It cost nothing to get in, I went through the back door...someone had left the back door open. I went to see Gary Glitter, and I couldn't get in the front at twelve! It was supposed to be over twenty-one at the door, but there were too many people inside to notice me.

Anon

In ballrooms, like the Grand Ballroom we used to have, there tended to be a lot of drink related bad behaviour which could be appalling and entirely upset one's weekend. And then of course people in a bigger hall, such as the Casino Club now, behave so well that there are only little bits of maintenance over the course of the year, perhaps amounting to only the replacement of hinges on doors and things like that, whereas if it was the ballroom it would be the whole door to be replaced!

E K Deeming

The Grand Ballroom — Rotarybanquet.

My brother "Mick" was an electrician to start with, then he was with the cinema a long time. When it was just me and my brother it was alright. We worked in with one another and he taught me the job.

When I first went, just after the war, on Mondays, you used to have a matinee. Tuesday mornings you had a thing for the pitmen, and Wednesdays you had a matinee in the afternoon and then the evening show. But, of course, just before it shut, you just had an evening show. Not many went to the miners' show, so that stopped, and if they wanted they'd have to go to the Wednesday one or in the evening. The curtains were lit up different colours — green, blue, all sorts. They were made of silvery coloured material.

It was a very long day. Of course you got home for dinner but you took your tea with you. They'd got a staff room but we stayed in the box. Once I got up in that box, I never came out unless I wanted to go to the toilet. There was a little porthole to watch the films. Most times we didn't because we threaded up and carbonned up and made sure it was all ready, and then went and wound the other film back ready for the next time. It was more difficult when they altered it to the big reels that took the whole picture. Before that the different parts of the picture were on different reels, on smaller spools. They altered it to just one reel for each picture. There were two sides on the projector, one for one picture and one for the other, when we had a double feature. Before the big reels, odd times, we'd get the spools mixed up.

There are some projectionists in other cinemas that are women but it's a dying art now.

S Charlton

The Rex Cinema, shortly after opening in February 1938.

There was nowhere else for people to go. We went Saturday and Sunday — special programme on Sundays — and the programme changed again on Wednesdays. You were too young to go in the pub so you went to the pictures.

It wasn't that you went to watch the films so much when you were courting, you just went because it was somewhere warm to go! It didn't really matter what was on.

M Sparrow.

There was the running board. After queuing, and there were no seats left, they would let you into the cinema. It was a board that ran all the way round the upstairs — a padded seat you could sit on. As seats became vacant the usherettes would take the first couple to a proper seat, but you were lucky sometimes if you didn't sit on the running board all night if it was a good film. We didn't mind.

There was a running board at the very back behind a wooden screen that finished off the back seats. You sat behind that but really the board was too high to look over and you stood up half the time. But at least you were in the cinema.

Another running board was just as you went into Coalville cinema where the staircase was. It ran round each side. I suppose it was like upstairs in the circle. Of course, the great attraction as you got older were the double seats at the back for the courting couples. There were about three or four rows of these. I remember when I was quite young, if we were bored with the film we'd turn round and watch what was going on behind. As you got older and advanced to the double seats you were busy telling them in front to turn round and mind their own business! You didn't want them looking while you were courting.

M Sparrow

The Rex, 1938.

Mr Lister came along in the post-war years, probably about 1948, as manager and persuaded my father to introduce a buffet counter. We had done catering as part of our interests in Loughborough and it was a very nice addition to the Rex.

E K Deeming

I used to use the Rex buffet quite often when I was unemployed, around about 1983, for a couple of years. It used to be a nice friendly place where they'd let you stay, over a cup of coffee, for anything up to three or four hours. It was the cheapest place in town and you could hide around some nice corners.

It was quite popular, especially around lunchtimes, with the people from Palitoy and there were a regular number of customers. There wasn't a fixed menu as such, just snacks, but people came in for coffee and tea. I think the coffee was about 15p and the tea 10p, but it was the cheapest place in town.

Anon

Coming from down south, I found it very strange to walk by people having tea and sandwiches to get to the pay box. Another thing I found strange was the amount of extra food people took in with them. Popcorn and sweets was quite normal, but crisps and packets of biscuits!!

V Parry

I was the first usherette to sell ice-cream at the Casino the very first night it opened, because they hadn't got anybody to sell it. I sold it in the interval at the Rex, then I had to put the tray down and run round to the Casino and do their sales as well.

Anon

The Rex Buffet, opened circa 1948.

The usherette's job was advertised in the paper so I went for it. She said, 'Can you start tonight?', and so I did. I went from quarter to five 'til ten and then I gradually got roped into the matinees and I was doing every matinee there was.

The film they showed when I first started was 'Annie Get Your Gun'. I've never seen so many people, there were queues and crowds of them, I couldn't get in! And I didn't know what to do. Nobody showed you anything, you had to pick it up for yourself.

The first thing we did when we got there was to put your uniform on, get your strings out for the tickets, find your torch, see that all the exit doors were right. Then you carried on, ripping tickets and going round with the ice-cream tray.

When I went to work there, there were about eight usherettes and two doormen. They all dwindled down 'til there was two of us when it finished but I was the only one on duty that night when it closed.

Anon

The Rex foyer, 1950s.

There was a lady in the box office who was there for as long as I can remember. She was quite strict. If there was a film on that we weren't old enough to see we would try and slip by.

M Sparrow

One night I was down by the front seats on what we use to call the 'sixpenny and ninepenny passage'. I was stood with my back to the screen looking up at the audience. There were a lot of youths kicking up a commotion. At this time I was chewing gum but with having false teeth it stuck to the top of them, to the plate. These youths got out of hand and I went to go up to them and then went to get rid of the chewing gum. I pulled my finger out of my mouth and out went my teeth with it! They went four or five rows up into the cinema. I went round all the seats, very near on my hands and knees, looking for my teeth. I couldn't find them. There was another girl there who took the ice-cream tray round and when she came back later she said, 'Look here, look what I've found.' My false teeth were in the tray.

Anon

The Rex foyer, showing the paybox, 1950s.

I remember seeing 'Rocky'. He started off very fat and unfit. Suddenly he was running up some steps, well on his way to being ready for the 'big fight'. The film continued with preparations for the fight and suddenly Rocky went back to being fat again. Then we watched him get reasonably fit and it jumped to the night of the fight. It made it quite interesting to see the film out of sequence although I would have preferred it in the right order.

V Parry

In Rex 1 we had 'American Werewolf in London' on a Sunday night. You used to have to watch for the change-overs. All of a sudden the werewolf was walking on the ceiling and the sound was all 'RRRRR' because it was obviously running upside down. Everyone thought it was funny at the time. In 'Privates on Parade' they all got off a bus before they got on it. I remember 'Grease'. The queue outside was so big I couldn't get in.

I'd start at 10am and we used to have a cat, Sheba, waiting to be fed, so that was the first job. Then we'd rewind the films, clean the projection room windows and do any odd jobs needing doing. I'd unlock the cinema doors. Then I'd light the Rex sign in the foyer, put the big fan on in Rex 1 and turn on all the balcony lights. Then into the projection room and put the emergency lights on, then switch all the house-lights on from there. Switch the projection machines on and leave them running for about a quarter of an hour to let the oil pump through them.

We used to thread them up, put the music on and about ten minutes before, strike the arc lights on and let them warm up.

J Knight

John Knight, projectionist 1978-1984.

I was there six years. It was different to working for the Rank Organisation and these chain cinemas because to them you were just a number. To the Deemings it was sort of like a family concern and once they knew you were trustworthy you were alright in it. I got on very well with Mr. Deeming.

J Knight

I had some good times there and I was very sorry when it closed. But the last night was ever so sad. There was so much ice-cream that had to be got rid of and they said, well, if you can't sell them, we'll give them away. So everybody who was in the cinema that night had a free ice-cream.

Anon

I brought the cat home when it finished, when the Rex closed. We had it here, and it was about two years ago when it died.

S Charlton

When the time came to go home we went in the office with Mr. Deeming and Mr. Gooding, the manager, and we had a drink of sherry and they said a few words. I was presented with a lovely basket of flowers and there was a taxi to bring me home. I thought, 'Well, that's the end of an era.'

Anon

The last picture show... video boom shuts Rex

By WENDY BADDLEY

COALVILLE'S only cinema closes its doors for the last time next Thursday, unable to compete with the video recorder boom.

And so too ends the Deeming family's involvement with cinemas in the town, which stretches back to 1920. At one time Coalville boasted three cinemas, all owned by the same family.

Audiences have been dropping steadily during the past couple of decades but the huge growth in video recorder ownership in the last year or so has forced the Rex to admit defeat.

"It is very sad," said managing director Mr Edward Deeming.

"The closure is purely economic. It simply is no longer commercially viable. It has been maintained and operated for some months at a loss.

"If it was not family owned it would probably have closed a couple of years ago. We have managed to extend its working life because of our personal involvement but we can no longer carry on. We are like any business organisation; our income needs to cover expenditure with a little to spare.

Converted

"Its decline is related directly to the national trend away from auditoria entertainment. We could compete with television but not video recorders.

"There are only about 1,300 cinemas left in this country — 30 years ago there were 3,500."

Mr Deeming's father, Charles Deeming, came to Coalville in 1920 and bought the Grand Cinema, which was converted into a dance hall after the Second World War and later sold. Now it is Bensons disco.

He also bought the Olympia which became known as the Regal in 1933. That was turned into the Casino Club in 1963.

The family built the Rex in 1938 and converted it into two smaller studios in 1974.

Now the Rex too is up for sale but Mr Deeming hopes to draw good sized audiences for its last week with two top films. Rex One is showing "Champions," starring John Hurt as jockey Bob Champion, who went on to win the Grand National after overcoming cancer. Rex Two is bringing back a name which is always popular; Clint Eastwood in the action-packed "Sudden Impact."

Edward Deeming outside the Rex, which is closing next week.

The Electricity Supply for this Cinema is generated by—

BRUSH
Diesel - Electric Plant

The installation consists of a BRUSH 4 Cylinder 136 B.H.P. Engine driving a BRUSH D.C. Generator. This Set complete with Switchboard was built at Falcon Works, Loughborough.

IF YOU ARE INTERESTED IN 'BRUSH' DIESELS, GENERATORS, MOTORS, TRANSFORMERS, CONVERTORS, WRITE TO
THE BRUSH ELECTRICAL ENGINEERING CO., LTD., LOUGHBOROUGH

"REX" PRESENTATIONS
For the month of FEBRUARY, 1938

WEDNESDAY, FEBRUARY 2nd (for Four Days):
"THE CHARGE OF THE LIGHT BRIGADE"

MONDAY, FEBRUARY 7th (Three Days):
MARLENE DIETRICH and CHARLES BOYER in
"THE GARDEN OF ALLAH"
also George O'Brien in "WHISPERING SMITH SPEAKS"

THURSDAY, FEBRUARY 10th (Three Days):
ERROL FLYNN in
"THE PRINCE AND THE PAUPER"

MONDAY, FEBRUARY 14th (Three Days):
CONRAD VEIDT and VIVIEN LEIGH in
"DARK JOURNEY"
also Jean Muir in "WHITE BONDAGE"

THURSDAY, FEBRUARY 17th (Three Days):
FLOTSAM AND JETSAM and a Host of Stars in
"CALLING ALL STARS"
also Buck Jones in "BLACK ACES"

MONDAY, FEBRUARY 21st (Three Days):
BASIL RATHBONE and ANN HARDING in
"LOVE FROM A STRANGER"

THURSDAY, FEBRUARY 24th (Three Days):
SABU in
"ELEPHANT BOY"
also Charles Quigley in "FIND THE WITNESS"

MONDAY, FEBRUARY 28th (Three Days):
JOE E. BROWN in
"POLO JOE"
also Hugh Williams in "THE PERFECT CRIME"

THURSDAY, MARCH 3rd (Three Days):
BORIS KARLOFF in
"NIGHT KEY"
also Paul Cavanagh in "CAFE COLLETTE"

CYCLE & CAR PARK

A Car Park is attached to the REX with entrance from Owen Street. It is under the supervision of a fully qualified Attendant with whom you may leave your Car or Cycle with safety. This Car Park will be FREE to the Patrons of the Rex, Regal or Grand.

TWENTY-ONE YEARS AGO

DO YOU REMEMBER . . . ?
the Opening Programme on February 2nd, 1938

Grand Opening Ceremony
by
Councillor T. E. Wand, J.P.
(Chairman, Coalville Urban District Council)

NEWS

"TREES" (A Rhapsody in Colour)

"THE CHARGE OF THE LIGHT BRIGADE"
with
ERROL FLYNN and OLIVIA DE HAVILLAND

(Stage Prologue by Mr. Fred Forgham)

God Save The King

SUCCESS STORY

Some of the outstandingly popular films that have been shown at the Rex

1938 A Star Is Born	1948 The Best Years of Our Lives
1939 The Drum	1949 Johnny Belinda
1940 Stagecoach	1950 Jolson Sings Again
1941 Convoy	1951 Annie Get Your Gun
1942 Dangerous Moonlight	1952 The Greatest Show on Earth
1943 The Road to Morocco	1953 The Cruel Sea
1944 Gone With The Wind	1954 From Here to Eternity
1945 Cover Girl	1955 The Robe
1946 The Way To The Stars	1956 Reach For The Sky
1947 Duel In The Sun	1957 The King And I

1958 The Bridge on The River Kwai

WALTER MOSS & SON

(Proprietor: ALWYN B. MOSS)

COALVILLE, Nr. LEICESTER

Telephone: COALVILLE 23

BUILDERS AND CONTRACTORS

Builders of this Cinema

Architect   HURLEY ROBINSON, F.R.I.B.A., A.I.S.E.

INLAND TELEGRAM

REX CINEMA STOP COALVILLE STOP LEICS STOP

CONGRATULATIONS ON YOUR MAJORITY STOP
MAY YOU CONTINUE FOR MANY MORE ENTERTAINING
YEARS STOP IN FACT DON'T STOP STOP
THE MAKERS OF  ICE CREAM

FOR ALL GRADES OF

MILK
Fresh Cream
Farm Eggs
Butter, etc.

PROMPT SERVICE AND CIVILITY

F. BIRD

FOREST ROAD
COALVILLE

Phone 592

C. V. LANE

PLUMBER

ASHBY ROAD
COALVILLE

Telephone 337 and 700

Coalville's Favourite Rendezvous
THE **REX** BUFFET

Reddings — Tea at its Finest

Served exclusively at the REX

Best wishes for the success of your Gala Performance from
REDDINGS TEA COMPANY LTD., of HAINAULT, ESSEX